Notable Moons

David Gunton

QUILLKEEPERS PRESS

ISBN:979-8-9868389-5-3

Published by Quillkeepers Press, LLC
PO Box 10236
Casa Grande, AZ 85130

This book is for Anne.

Table of Contents

I.

II.

I.

Bed of Reeds

You came into this world the same way
We all did, on the banks of an enormous
Freshwater lake, your father somewhere off in the brush,
Searching for this herb or that, for the ceremonial
Burning, deaf to the calls of the midwives,
The seven midwives, announcing that the moment
Drew near, crowded around your mother,
Seated on a bed of reeds, eyes fixed on
The horizon, on a boat, a rock, a lone cloud.

The Townspeople

We live in primitive times. It's obvious
From the traffic signals, from the varieties
Of cleansers available in the grocery stores,
From the grocery stores themselves, primitive structures,
Rectangles, a crude shape, elemental.

Walk into the street and make a primitive sound,
A shout or yelp. Likely as not, someone
Will shout right back at you, multiple someones.
Likely as not, the townspeople will find it
Wholly unremarkable. The primitive townspeople.

Notable Moons

The crickets are at it again. The cars
Are rolling down Broadway. The trees are just
Standing there, waiting for the show to begin.
The bats take flight, from one end of the yard
To the other. The moon rises. It's a harvest moon
Or a blood moon or a super moon. It's
A notable moon. The lamp sheds light.
The furniture takes up its space in the room.
The window is open. The Queen is dead.
The spiders crawl forth and spin their webs.

Beach Scenes

The lamp sheds light. Your makeshift bed
Lies on the floor, unceremoniously,
Each of the rooms occupied by someone
Nursing one sickness or another.
The sewing bin has been left open, the masks
Are strewn about. The armchair is occupied
By a pile of stuffed sloths. Family pictures
Line the mantle. Beach scenes, babies
In swaddling clothes. Mom and Dad
Striding confidently toward the camera.

The Kettle Won't Boil

Family pictures line the mantle
And no one is coming down the chimney.
You take up your position by the window
And wait for the leaves to start to turn,
Understanding, that without your
Patient observation, time will not march on,
No one will come home, not another car
Will roll down the street, the kettle
Won't boil, the tea won't steep, the wind,
Your oldest friend, won't pay its daily call.

A Playbill, A Candle

You made an inventory of all the things
Out of place. One can of WD40,
Left on a bin of puzzles. A matchbox car
In the middle of the floor. One air mattress,
Sheets, and a pillow, arrayed in front
Of the fireplace. Yesterday's clothes
Strewn across a chair. Two pair
Of slippers. Three high school yearbooks.
A playbill, a candle. A red pincushion
With a pox of pins of green and gold.

Pancakes

Waffle was the word that escaped you
And then it was *Screwdriver*, then *Pillow*,
Then *Pair*. But you could get along
Without these things very well. It was nothing
To you to have pancakes for breakfast.
To tighten your bolts with a steel Allen wrench, why,
You must have half a dozen around here.
To sleep on a stuffed bear, you snagged
From the attic. To walk to the kitchen,
Open a drawer, and set a table for one.

Two Kinds

There are two kinds of people in this world
And you weren't either one of them.
You were just a rolling stone, to coin a phrase,
A bird on a wire, if you will, a barbed wire surrounding
A municipal lot of empty buses and trains,

Out of commission, and that could be you too
Down there, walking from car to car, charged
With washing the graffiti off the sides,
Pausing each time, unsure of how to proceed,
In the presence of all that beauty.

Basic Ruins

Alone then, in the high school auditorium,
One flagpole on the far left side
Of the stage, one flag, the enormous
Red velvet curtains, hung from the ceiling,
Drawn to a close, concealing behind them
The cardboard facade of a pirate ship,
A chrome lunch counter and three pink stools,
A horse costume, a goat costume, a pedestal
That could denote Ancient Greece, or just
Your basic ruin, someone stumbled upon.

Your Number

The will to live weakened. Nothing
Dramatic. Just a little softer around
The edges, a little slower out of the gate.
The absurd scenarios you imagined
When you were young, the burning building,
The plummeting plane—the maniacal lengths
You would go to survive, now it struck you:
Would it really be worth all that trouble,
The inconvenience to yourself and others?
For, after all, when it's your number.

Last Stop

It was the hour of owls. Autumnal Equinox.
Last stop on the train. Shoppers parading
Down the streets and buying things that aren't
For sale. It was a quiet time. A summarizing
Of a great many things. A moon that rose in the sky
And for once just stayed there. It was a full moon.
A tilt of the head and a flick of the wrist.
Code words written in twigs and leaves, some of them
In sand. Spiders on the move. It was when spiders
Would spin their webs, strike them, spin them again.

The Sunken City

They say a sunken city lies beneath
The lake, that a stranger asked the people
For help one day, that he was turned away,
That he placed his curse upon the city,
That the rain started slowly at first,
Steady and unremarkable, a mild
Inconvenience, that it began to draw comment,
That the market flooded first, that one family
Then another decided to flee, that many stayed
And stared at the water, falling and falling.

Companions

You never step in the same river twice
But your feet get wet every time
As you stagger out onto the bank
And into a dark and quiet wood,
Like something out of one of those fairy tales,
You observed to your traveling companion,
Your second-grade teacher, you just
Happened to see her, on the side of the road,
The pink hibiscus bloom in her gray bun
Catching your eye, you said, hop in.

An Appraisal

An appraisal of the sideboard: two lamps
Ordered online, a sheet of loose-leaf paper
With a child's writing, a pencil sharpener,
Electric, loud, a miniature lightboard
For whimsical messages, two dinner napkins,
Discarded, a purple stylus with a purple-haired
Doll's head on the top, a smartphone face down,
A little easel for displaying a photograph,
A candle bought dearly, basil and lime,
Fashioned of beeswax, waiting its turn.

The Banana Plant

A found hour in the City, quickly you procured
A donut, a cup of tea, a bottle of water
And continued walking south until you found
One of those parks in the middle of the street,
A table for two, traffic on all sides and trees
Overhead, the pigeons sitting six to a branch,
The branches having seen this one before,
And now it's starting to rain, but not to worry, Dad,
The leaves of the banana plant in the terracotta pot
Are more than enough to cover you both.

Portrait

Hand-held vacuum cleaner, perched
Upright, atop its charging base,
Nose pointed to the ceiling, man
Of all work, furtive accomplice,
At once a relic of a bygone era
And a perfection of the form,
Nasty brute, the clear suggestion
Of a rodent, large, aquatic,
Its habitat far closer than imagined,
Its intelligence a matter of interest.

Cherubs and Horses

A jewel thief dresses all in black
Traditionally, an all-black ensemble
Close-fitting at the shoulders and hips
With a black knit cap, ample enough
To tuck inside one's long auburn hair
As final preparations are made
Before a vanity, Louis XVI,
One with a gilt frame featuring carvings
Of cherubs and horses, intricate
Carvings depicting one Biblical story,
Or another.

The Simple Rapture

We couldn't do anything to stop
The destruction, so we turned it into
An entertainment, reclined in our chairs
And watched debris blow down the street,
Trees bend then break, lamps explode.

Others preferred the human drama,
The rending and wailing, but our tastes were more
Toward property damage. The floating car,
The bridge collapse, the simple rapture
Of watching the whole reduced to the many.

II.

Saw Mill River

1.

Mugwort, knotweed, loosestrife,
Saluting the gurgling waters.
The glaciers rolled down and then receded.
A girl skips a stone on a fallen beam.

Ginger, dandelion, garlic mustard,
Thornwood, Hawthorne, City of Yonkers.
Pull eleven logs fast, wrap them in rope,
Sail your raft to the mouth of the river.

2.

Mind the eels. They start in the Harbor,
Follow their stars north to Yonkers
And embark upstream, thousands of eels
Past Hastings, Hawthorne, Pocantico,

Past mugwort, bittersweet, Queen Anne's lace.
They routed and re-routed the river.
They buried the river and raised it again.
They spoiled the river, and still, the eels.

3.

River of ghosts, the tribes that camped
And decamped, the Dutch who dropped their lines
In Colendonck's Kill, in Saeck's kill,
The English, Hessians, Wappinger Nation,

They walk the banks. Too many ghosts.
In the morning mist, it's common to see them.
The glaciers rolled down and then receded.
Roll down again and free these spirits.

4.

It's a haunted river. The Put rumbles in
To Mount Hope Station, and the mourners march,
Follow the coffin in a purple carriage.
Trains of mourners and trains of orphans.

One more stop, off at Chauncey, one more hill,
The opposite hill, straight up now past rock and crag,
The City's children, don't look back.
Don't look down at the little river.

5.

On the bank of the river, the horse
Of the headless horseman, stooping to drink,
The rider milling about in the mist
Just hovering above the water's surface

Reams of knotweed poking through
Mugwort, bittersweet, honeysuckle.
One egret, wary of these two, not ready
To quit the scene just yet, thank you.

6.

Take the counsel of a double-crested cormorant
Cooling himself in Woodlands Lake,
Apart and ignored by a flock of ducks,
Wading among the algae and kelp.

Scummy lake, the impounded river,
Keeping his distance from the waterfall,
Paying no mind to the log or the turtle
Receiving no greeting in return.

7.

Route, then re-route the river.

Find the path that suits your needs.

Bury, then dig up the river.

You decide where there will be light.

Spoil, then purify the river.

Throw everything in you want to forget.

Name, then rename the river.

Let your present replace your past.

8.

It was a simple estate, with few
Beneficiaries. He left his gardener's tools
To the boy at the end of the cul-de-sac.
He left his sailor's hat to an Aunt Jane.

He left his silverware and flatware
To the Episcopal Church. He left
Clear instructions that his class ring, watch,
And locket all be thrown into the river.

9.

Be that piece of driftwood
Drifting past Eastview and Elmsford
Now past Getty Square, under the tracks
Into the Hudson, now under the bridge

Into the harbor, you are past the Battery
Around Coney Island, so many lights
You are bobbing with the swans now in Sheepshead Bay,
You are remembering life in the river.

10.

It fell upon you to sort the belongings.
Half a pack of Uno cards.
An iPad, dead and out of date.
A book on yoga for beginners.

Historical photographs, alphabetized,
Of Twentieth Century factories.
A twenty-piece puzzle, ages two and up.
A pencil sketch he made of the river.

The Upholstery

The rock wall is a clock
Ticking so loudly
So reliably, you can hardly
Hear yourself think sometimes
Sitting in your mauve armchair
Just able to see a section
Of the face, through the oak
And maple leaves, the section
Expanding as the leaves fall,
The upholstery faded and torn.

A Distant Star

You returned to your car and found it
Surrounded by deer, a doe and two fawns
In a loose semicircle, a promising sign
Perhaps, the animal spirit, rebirth,
Fertility, the changing of the seasons,
Or was it, no, something more ominous,
Nature displaced and now on a journey
To parts unknown, unknowable to you,
Traveling under a distant star, you try
To find it, but, to you, they all look the same.

The Mountain

You decided to leave everything behind
For a bit, and hike the mountain, and so did
Everyone else, you were shoulder to shoulder
On the trail, your view blocked by a man
With a child in his backpack. You stopped
At a stop where they were selling t-shirts,
Canteens, and playing cards depicting the mountain.
You bought a t-shirt, and a coffee, and sat down next
To a fellow hiker. We live in primitive times,
He said, and he had that faraway look in his eyes.

Acknowledgments

Thank you, Henry, Sam, Nancy, and Justin, for your guidance and friendship, and thank you, Stephanie and Dylan, for believing in this book.

About the Author

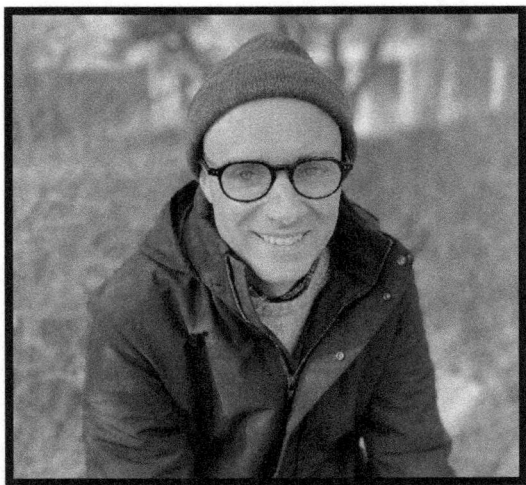

David Gunton's writing has appeared in La Petite Zine, The Long Island Quarterly, and The Oxford Encyclopedia of American Literature, among other publications. He is also the co-author, along with Justin Hendrix, of "Poegles: A Short History and Collection." He has lived in Ohio, Virginia, Washington, D.C., New York, and Georgia, and now resides with his family in the Hudson Valley.

What Others are Saying About Notable Moons

Notable Moons, Dave Gunton's welcome debut collection, evokes William Carlos Williams's "Spring and All [By the road to the contagious hospital]" in its meditative, sure-footed cataloging of lost and discarded objects that choke the beautiful Indian rivers of our nation. In "Saw Mill River," a stunning poem in ten sections, the poet calls forth the tribes that once camped along this misused "River of ghosts," followed by a succession of European invaders. Despite the broken, innumerable objects thrown into the river or left behind by the living and the dead, Nature refuses to be defeated —the ever-present crickets, bats taking flight, the astonishing face of the Blood Moon rising. You will love this book.

—Nancy Schoenberger, author of *Long Like a River* (poetry) and *Dangerous Muse* (a biography of Caroline Blackwood)

Notable Moons is notable for its meditative poems of "patient observation"—to borrow a phrase from one of the poems. Like Li Po or Tu Fu, David Gunton observes ordinary life with clarity, compassion, and humor. By doing so, he shows us how to cope with the all-too-familiar upheavals that he also observes: pandemics, environmental disasters, terrorist attacks, deaths of admired leaders. This is an impressive first book that should appeal to all readers of poetry.

—Henry Hart, author of *Rooster Mask* and former Poet Laureate of the State of Virginia

www.ingramcontent.com/pod-product-compliance
Lightning Source LLC
Chambersburg PA
CBHW022106020426
42335CB00012B/859